MW00470330

YOU CAN'T GET THERE FROM HERE

How To Get To A Better Life

El Shaddai Christian Assembly
1448 Greenwood Avenue,
Philadelphia Pennsylvania 19150
Website: www.elsca.org
Email: pastor2210@elsca.org

Unless otherwise indicated, all Scripture quotations are taken
from the *New King James Version* of the Bible.

Cover and page layout by M.A. Jones Designs

ISBN 978-0-9973324-0-7
Library of Congress #2016936459

Printed in the United States of America.

YOU CAN'T GET THERE FROM HERE

FROM HERE

How To Get To A Better Life

JAMES E. WOODS

CONTENTS

DEDICATION

This book is dedicated to my wife, Barbara, who has both supported and encouraged me for over 38 years. She continues to be an example of integrity and character for me, our children and grandchildren. I thank God for blessing me with this wonderful woman.

ACKNOWLEDGE

I would like to thank God for His goodness toward me. My son, James Woods III, and my daughter, Tiffany (Woods) Ifon. Both of whom have encouraged me to write and suffered through years of my procrastination. To Dr. Patricia Powell, who would not take no for an answer and her vision to provoke all believers to write books. I am grateful for her persistence, willingness to travel and her editing of this book. To Terri Hayes for helping create an environment that facilitated the writing process. To my brother, John Cooper, who took time away from his doctoral studies to both read the book and write the forward. And to all the members of El Shaddai Christian Assembly, whose prayers and support have blessed me through the years.

Pastor James E. Woods II
July 2015

FORWARD

When my brother, Pastor James E. Woods, told me he was writing this book, I was excited to hear that he was finally going to put a portion of his wealth of knowledge onto paper. I believed there are several benefits to this writing, one being it will be available for all to read, and another is it will allow him to leave a legacy for many generations to come. For many years I often referred to James as one of the most intelligent people I know. He is usually the first person I call when I have a question about life, bible, or spiritual matters. I have been truly blessed having had such a resource in my life. Having a big brother with so many intellectual talents wasn't always easy with me being the competitive type. I grew up determined to challenge Jim in a few areas. These challenges forced me to become a rather savvy chess player, as he is one of the best at the game. It also was the driving force that lead me to a doctoral study of education at Grand Canyon University.

As Pastor Woods' youngest brother, I have watched him succeed in many areas; with a tenacious desire to win and to accomplish a vast number of things, he takes many challenges head on. Like most people, James has had many setbacks in life; however, in observing him over the years, I have learned it's not what happens to you in life, but how you deal with what happens that will determine the outcome.

This book was designed to help individuals like yourself to turn your life around and to get where you want to go. This book provides the recipe for changing the direction of your life and helping readers to understand that you are in control of your destiny. In this book, you will learn the steps needed to first evaluate yourself and discover where you are presently. The second step is to figure out where you want to be. The third step is discovering the path and direction of how to get "THERE".

The writer of this book brings a wealth of knowledge with over 30-years of pastoral and counseling experience. This book was written to fill a need that was discovered. Pastor Woods noticed there were many people trying to find themselves and trying to figure out how they arrived in the place called "HERE". He desires to help all that want help to escape from the place called "HERE" to finally get "THERE". However, in order to make this transition you must be willing to make several drastic and immediate changes. By following and applying the information from this book you will be surprised how different your life will be when you are free.

Where are you today? Think in terms of physically, emotionally, spiritually, and financially. If you cannot honestly say you are happy with all of these areas of your life, then this is indeed the book for you. The goal of this book is to see you succeed in every aspect of your life. At no point in this book will the author tell you it will be easy; however, the good news is that succeeding in every area of your life is not impossible. This book has now become a great tool in my life as a gauge for moving forward in the right direction.

Are you willing to make some changes in your life? Are you willing to be committed to change? If your answer is yes you may continue to read. Getting started today is the key; don't procrastinate. One thing I have learned over the years is when someone is serious and committed they begin immediately. Do not put off starting until tomorrow, next week, or next month;' instead begin your journey today.

John R. Cooper, MBA
Grand Canyon University, Doctoral Studies
Philadelphia, PA
July 2015

1

YOU CAN'T GET THERE
FROM HERE

> Young man walks into a bar after a hard day's work, sits down on a stool and asks for a drink. Bartender serves him his first drink. He downs it quickly and asks for a second drink. He repeats this process three more times. After a while the young man now intoxicated wants to talk. He asked the bartender "Do you know how to get to heaven?" The bartender replies "The only thing I'm sure of, young man, is that you cannot get there from here." -J. Woods

Many people today may not find themselves sitting on a barstool questioning how to get to heaven, but they do wonder how to get somewhere that will provide them a better life. The problem is that they find themselves in a place called "HERE" and want to get to a place called "THERE", not knowing how to get there.

Before you can learn how to get to "THERE" you must first ascertain how you got "HERE". While you may think that the answer to that question is complicated, it may be simpler than you think. Truth of the matter is, you worked very hard to get "HERE".

You arrived here as a result of the sum total of your belief system, your thinking, decisions you have made or allowed to be made for you, and the actions you have taken. Now, if you are satisfied with being "HERE", then this book is not for you. This book is dedicated to those who want to get out of "HERE".

To succeed in this endeavor is going to require being completely honest with yourself. You will not be allowed to blame your current situation on the parenting skills of your mother and father. Nor will you be able to accuse society, your race, the neighborhood you grew up in or your third grade math teacher. You are going to need a notebook and pencil because I'm going to ask you to write down some very important information at the beginning so that we can finish this journey. You not only will realize how you got out of "HERE", but hopefully you'll be able to help someone else as well.

2

THE CITY CALLED "HERE"

"Here" is unusual among cities in that there are no roads connecting the city to the rest of the country (although ferry service is available for cars). The absence of a road network is due to the extremely rugged terrain surrounding the city. This in turn makes "Here" a de-facto island city in terms of transportation, since all goods coming in and out must go by plane or boat, in spite of the city being located on the mainland. Downtown "Here" sits at sea level, with tides averaging 16 feet (5 m), below steep mountains about 3,500 feet (1,100 m) to 4,000 feet (1,200 m) high. Atop these mountains are the ice fields, a large ice mass from which glaciers flow and which are visible from the local road system.

"Here" is over crowded, Each year multitudes moved into the city but only a handful move out. The racial makeup of the city is equally dispersed with people of all ethnic backgrounds. Most of the people are content with their living arrangements, and many of the people earned a decent income, but they would also admit to earning less than their potential.

Downtown "Here" boasts dozens of shops , art galleries, specialty shops, and many other types of businesses that would make living in "Here" comfortable and convenient. Friday evenings open-air music and dance performances are held in the Park. Every effort has been made to convince the citizens of "Here" to remain. It has tree-lined streets, movie theaters, even a casino.

The two largest and busiest streets are, Standard of Living Boulevard, and Career Avenue. The streets are paved with asphalt and have cement sidewalks and plenty of traffic lights. They boast some of the best shopping in town. You can buy everything from accounting services to lottery tickets. Some of the nicest homes (heavily mortgaged) and cars can be found on these two streets. However, there are no travel agencies or career opportunity centers to be found on either of the streets. In fact, there are no travel agencies or career centers in the whole city. The flagship institutions at both ends, are the shopping malls and the casinos. Tourists even visit "Here", mostly by cruise ship, and are mainly foreigners. When asked why they visit "Here", most of the foreigners want to see people who live in such a great country, but choose to live in the city of "Here".

In fact, on the surface it seems like a great place to live. "Here" is a trap to subtly convince its citizens that this is the best life they could have. "Here" has all the modern conveniences, but secretly offers no real opportunities for improvement. The real secret of "Here" is that nothing ever improves or changes. In recent interviews with the citizens of "Here", most were not happy with living here, but after several attempts to leave they gave up in despair. Several went on to say "It is not that bad, if you can accept a substandard life. You get use to it."

The city of "Here" is a bigger travesty, because it is across the bay from unlimited opportunity. It is amazing how many people come from other parts of the world and clearly recognize the opportunities that exist so close to "Here". On the other hand, people who live in "Here" wonder how foreigners do so well just across the bay. The answer is simple: they have escaped the city of "Here" in their own country, and set sail for the shining city of "There". Sad to say, the people of "Here", while living close to "There", are stuck in the one city that limits their opportunities. If they would only recognize that the city of "Here" is more a state of mind than a physical location, they could escape. I trust that you, as the reader of this book, will come to realize the trap this malicious city offers, and seek the path of escape.

While the city is mythical, the condition of state of mind is not. Each year amid an endless array of circumstances, millions of people find themselves moving to the city called "Here". Unfortunately, many educational systems and political systems have a vested interest in increasing the population of "Here". The more people stranded in "Here", the more dependent they are on government and politicians to ease their discontent. This in turn produces bigger government, which limits the power of the individual at the expense of personal freedom.

One nation's founding father said, "Anyone willing to give up freedom for security will end up with neither". Unfortunately, this is the most dangerous aspect of the city of "Here". It gives the false impression that everything is safe and secure. Isolated from the damage that big government spending is causing, the people of "Here" continue to endorse or support through ignorance the very people, policies and institutions that will eventually destroy all the opportunities the country offers.

Why do people who are unhappy or dissatisfied remain in the city of "Here"? The answer is fear. Fear immobilizes people and prevents them from taking the necessary steps to escape. Fear causes people to think irrationally about their situation and possible solutions. Fear disrupts the normal mechanisms that would empower people to change. Fear is insidious because it operates both overtly and covertly. The key to overcoming fear is thinking rationally and taking action; i.e., do it while you are afraid. Think, what is the worst thing that could happen? Then what? You go on.

When you take action the, first thing you will discover is that fear yields. So make that commitment, register for the class, apply for the position, shop for that new home, even while your mind is screaming "But what if?"

I used to have an irrational fear of talking to strangers on the phone. My wife used words to help me overcome this fear. She said " What are you afraid of? They can't beat you or eat you". The next time I had to call a stranger, I said to myself, "You cannot beat me, and you cannot eat me" and the fear was gone.

3

WHERE IS HERE?

"Here" is where you find yourself today at this moment in your life physically, emotionally, financially, socially, and spiritually. It is more than just your geographical locations in terms of longitude and latitude. It is also where you find yourself regarding your attitudes, ambitions,and desire or lack thereof. "Here" is where you are today as a result of what you believe, how you think, the decisions you have made and the actions you have taken. Unless you modify your beliefs, improve the way you think, and make some decisions different than those you've made in the past "Here" is where you'll be tomorrow. The question you need to ask yourself is, "Do I like it HERE?"

Now, if you like it here, and by like I do not mean you're okay here, then there's no need for you to continue. But if you have no desire to stay in this place called "Here",and would like to transition your life from where it is today, then mark your calendar, because on this day at this time you are making the decision to escape from HERE!

Before you begin, you must take an inventory or bearings of your present location. To do this you will need to make a list of facts concerning the current areas of your life. Identify and list your present status physically i.e. your health, emotionally. That is to say are you happy, satisfied,or at peace? Financially, are you earning as much as you would like to? Do you have enough money saved, or are you deep in debt and struggling to make ends meet? How are your relationships with your spouse, siblings, children, neighbors, or coworkers? Last but certainly not least spiritually. How is your relationship with the God of creation and his only means of salvation, his son Jesus Christ? Are you actively involved with and committed in the church fellowship? Do you attend services on a regular basis?

As you assess all these areas of your life, be open and honest with yourself. Identify the areas that you are pleased with and feel that if they remained as they are today you would be okay. You can work on those last. But, bear in mind that even these areas have room for improvement.

There is one truth that you're going to have to accept if you are going to escape from HERE. You have arrived at your current locale because of YOU! Very few people find themselves in situations because of events that were totally beyond their control. Most people are in debt because they spent the money, are in low paying jobs because of education or bad choices they've made in the past or because of how they chose to conduct themselves in relationships.

The goal of this book is not to pile a ton of blame on you for everything that's wrong with your life, but it is focused on getting you to accept responsibility for where you are today. Because if you are willing to accept all responsibility for where you are, you can also take credit for where you are headed. While it is true the ultimate success in life consists of several factors, among them being the grace of God, relationships with others, and self-determination, you will discover that your role in this is much greater than you believe. Just like when you wake up in the morning it is you who determine what clothes you wear, whether or not you eat breakfast, or how you get to work, it is also you who has a lot to say about in what direction your life is headed and how you get there. Some of the things which you will be asked to do will be difficult and challenging for you to do more than others. But in order to achieve what others have not, you must be willing to do what others will not. In order to see what others have not seen you must be willing to look at what others will not.

A huge crowd was watching the famous tightrope walker, Blondin, cross Niagara Falls one day in 1860. He crossed it numerous times—a 1,000 foot trip, 160 feet above the raging waters. He asked the crowd if they believed he could take one person across. All assented. Then he approached one man and asked him to get on his back and go with him. The man refused! Mental assent or even verbal assent is not real belief.

Tan, P. L. (1996). Encyclopedia of 7700 Illustrations: Signs of the Times (p. 185). Garland, TX: Bible Communications, Inc.

It is also important for you to understand that as the author of this work, I have a vested interest in your success. If as the result of your reading this book, doing the exercises, and following the principles you still find yourself stuck in a place called HERE, then I have not achieve the purpose for which I have written it. However, if you don't do the exercises, skip pages and try to take a shortcut, you know why you are still stuck in "Here"!

What you believe has a major influence on how you think, and because we are the governor of our thought processes, it is important to take a few moments to discuss the issue of what you believe, and why you will need to modify some of your beliefs if you truly desire to escape from "HERE"

First you need to make a distinction between belief and mental assent. There are many things that you will mentally and verbally go along with, but do not believe them or have confidence enough to be persuaded by them. The difference between belief and mental assent is your willingness to act. Just as the illustration above, when it comes time to act the distinction becomes quite clear. You are not in your current situation because of what you mentally assented to but, you are here in part because of which you believed, to the extent that you were willing to act upon it. Your belief system has control and is influencing your thought processes and will continue to do so.

Questions:

1) What parallels do you see between the mythical city of "Here" in the real world?

2) Is there anything about the city that you see in your life?

3) List three reasons you think people would stay in the city.

4) Why do you think you have stayed "Here" so long?

5) What demographic from the city do you fit in?

6) What would be the political impact if all the citizens of "Here" started leaving?

7) What policies would a politician who wanted to help people leave the city of "Here" want to change or abolish?

4

DEAD END

In the city of "Here" you will find two types of streets: the first Street takes you in a circle, the second Street leads to a dead end. The basic truth about living in "Here" is that anytime you traveling you are either going in circles or heading toward a dead end. You would think that in this case many people would be fed up and ask for directions to leave. However, there is a certain degree of comfort in knowing that you can never be lost in "Here". So, for many people this becomes their comfort zone, and the thought of leaving is more frightening.

The two largest and busiest streets in "Here" are Standard of Living Boulevard and Career Avenue. Both these streets run parallel to each other, and they both dead-end at the same point. The ironic thing is that the speed limit on both of these streets is 55 mph. The other oddity about both the streets is that there is a casino at one end of both streets and shopping malls at the opposite ends.

It is amazing that when people feel they have reached a dead-end, they will either put their confidence in luck, or soothe the despair with debt. Either way these actions do nothing to help them get out of "Here".

The question is, Are you in debt? Do you play the lottery? Once you are taking the proper actions to escape from "Here", you will not have to rely on luck or to soothe your despair with debt. As a matter-of-fact you will begin to delight in saving money and creating your own opportunities that are sure things, unlike the lottery.

Questions:

1) Do you gamble or play the lottery? If so how much have you spent over the last three years?

2) Do you have any credit cards that are currently at their limit?

3) When was the last time you bought something you knew you could not afford?

4) When was the last time you got a raise that was not the result of a cost-of-living adjustment?

5) When was the last time you got a promotion?

6) If you could change your career, what would you change to?

7) Have you ever had the feeling that you had reached a dead end?

5

SLAP STREET

A terrible blizzard was raging over the eastern United States making more and more difficult the progress of a train that was slowly pacing its way along.

Among the passengers was a woman with a child, who was much concerned lest she should not get off at the right station. A gentleman, seeing her anxiety, said:"Do not worry. I know the road well, and I will tell you when you come to your station."

In due course the train stopped at the station before the one at which the woman wanted to get off."The next station will be yours, ma'am," said the gentleman.

Then they went on, and in minutes the train stopped again.

"Now is your time, ma'am; get out quickly," he said.

The woman took up her child, and thanking the man, left the train. At the next stop, the brakeman called out the name of the station where the woman had wished to get off.

"You have already stopped at this station," called the man to the brakeman. "No, sir." he replied, "Something was wrong with the engine, and we stopped for a few moments to repair it!"

"Alas!" cried the passenger, "I put that woman off in the storm when the train stopped between stations!" Afterwards, they found her with her child in her arms. Both were frozen to death! It was the terrible and tragic consequence of wrong direction being given! Still more terrible are the results of misdirecting souls!

—Billy Sunday

Can you tell me how to get to Slap Street? This was beginning to one of my uncle's favorite stunts. He would drive up to total strangers and asked them for directions to a street that did not exist. The thing that amazed me is how often people would attempt to provide answers and directions to a mythical street. It was a rare individual who would say "I have no idea where Slap Street is". This taught me a very powerful lesson at a very early age. People will try to help you even if the help is totally wrong.

This is important information to have if you desire is to escape from "Here". You see, the last person you should ask for directions for how to escape from "Here" is someone who lives "Here". Because while they may have the grandest intentions, if they really knew how to leave "Here" why are they still here?

One of the first lessons that you will need to learn, if you desire to turn your life around is to get information, counsel and advice from people who are where you want to be. This means you are going have to connect with people outside of your circle of acquaintances or your comfort zone. You may have to read books you have not read, talk to people you do not know and connect with groups/ organizations with which you are not identified at present. Time is too short and life is too precious to make decisions based on bad information.

If you have done the evaluations we discussed in previous chapters, you now have a clear understanding of where it is you desire to go. The next step is to educate yourself regarding your future destination. If

Tan, P. L. (1996). Encyclopedia of 7700 Illustrations: Signs of the Times (pp. 492–493). Garland, TX: Bible Communications, Inc.

it is a change in career, you need to collect information on how to prepare for that new career. You need to know the educational requirements and technical skills or experiences an employer in that career field would be seeking. If it is dealing with debt, you will need to educate yourself on how to manage your finances and proper budgeting. This can be resolved through reading books or taking classes addressing those issues. If the place you want to go to involves relationships, you will need to learn proper social skills and learn to communicate and socialize with other people. In other words, before you can leave Here, you will need to learn some things. There is an old adage which says, "To have what others do not have, you must do what others will not do." There is a reason so many people live in "Here", and are unwilling or lack motivation to do what it takes. Because you are reading this book, that statement no longer applies to you.

Because we live in an age of modern technology and unlimited access to information such as a computer, iPad or Smart phone, you can access information on any subject at any time. You, my friend, are blessed to live in a day and age where there is no excuse for being stranded in "Here". You can start today researching all the information you need to know about a place called "There". Because if "There" is where you want to be, you need to have a crystal clear image of what it looks like and how the inhabitants of "There" live and act.

Questions:

1) Have you ever asked someone for directions and they turned out to be wrong?

2) Have you ever asked and got bad advice from friends?

3) Who are three people you go to when you need help or information?

4) If you do not know something where is the first place you look?

6

AFRAID TO FLY

Scrawled in a nervous hand across a blackboard at Southern Methodist University during finals week was this message: "We have nothing to fear, but fear itself."

I still remember the first time I travel by air. I was traveling with a group of friends to Los Angeles, California. We were attending an event celebrating the life of a minister we all knew quite well. When some friends and associates heard I was traveling by plane, they asked me if I was afraid to fly. I informed them that not only was I not afraid to fly, I was looking forward to it. At that point they shared with me all the possible dangers associated with flying.

Since this was my first flight, I did not know what to expect. We left Philadelphia International Airport at midnight, the "redeye" to the Dallas Fort Worth Airport. Upon arrival we were required to transfer to a connecting flight going to Los Angeles. The problem was as I headed toward the connecting gate I noticed everyone was running in the direction of my gate. Now, I have seen enough monster pictures to know that if everyone is running, you run first and ask why everyone is running later. So I ran, only to discover there was no monster in the airport! The airline had overbooked the flight, and everyone was running to get a seat, which was on a first-come first-served basis. By the way, I am not afraid to fly, but monsters are another issue altogether.

With 3/5 of the Earth's surface being covered by water, flying or sailing are the only two ways you will get to see most of it. A fear of flying limits the size and scope of your world. The reality is people are not afraid to fly, they are afraid to die. But, if you think about it, most people who die in airplanes, die when the plane hits the ground not when it is in the air. In any given year more people die in their sleep than while flying. But I have yet to have one of my friends tell me they were afraid to go to sleep.

The reason why I mentioned flying at this point is because it is one of only two ways you can escape from "Here". The reality is all the streets in "Here" run either in a circle or to a dead-end. You will not be driving or riding your bicycle out of "Here". Consequently, there are only two ways to fly: either fly yourself or pay someone else to fly you. To fly yourself you will need access to a plane, and a pilot's license. To acquire both of these will cost you a lot. To pay someone else to fly you will also cost. Put simply, it is going to cost you to get out of "Here".

To fly in this case is being used metaphorically to represent elevating your thinking and believing. This process can only be achieved by exploring new and better information. It is going to require you to invest time and money in researching, investigating and acquiring new information. If you are in debt, you will have to seek out information on how to better manage your money. If you have relationship issues, you have to acquire information on how to better relate to others. (Please note this assumes that your relationship issues have just as much to do with you as much as with those around you. But, they are not reading this book; you are.) Whatever life issues are responsible for your being stranded in "Here", you are going to have to change how you think in order to be free.

Questions:

1) List three things you are afraid of or hesitate to do.

2) Have you ever been on an airplane or a cruise ship? If you have never been on either of these, why not?

3) When was the last time you visited someplace new?

4) When was your last vacation and how long did it last?

5) When is your next vacation?

6) What is the farthest you ever traveled from home and how long did you stay?

7) Would you be willing to travel to some place in the next year?

7

THE WORLD IS FLAT

Paradigm Shift *(noun)* 1. a radical change in underlying beliefs or theory

> Ralph Waldo Emerson was correct in asserting, "Man is what he thinks about all day long." That which he or she feeds on, the context of his/her experience, the playbacks from previous contacts, all have frightening and sometimes wonderful means of shaping and strengthening life.

It was once commonly believed that the world was flat. Following this logic it is rational to believe it was possible to fall off the edge. This misconception limited the size of the world,and led people to believe they had seen it all. But, when people, such as Christopher Columbus, challenged the status quo it led to the discovery of a whole new world. This new world was filled with wonders and riches beyond anything, anyone could hope for.

Is your world flat? Is your world limited to all that you can see? I want to challenge you to answer three questions

1. If money were not an issue, where would you go and what would you do differently?

2. If you have access to the greatest library what would you research?

3. If you could have any career or business you

desire, what would it be, and how much would you earn?

When you answer these questions, do not cheat yourself!

Questions:

1) When was the last time you changed your mind about something important?

2) What do you now believe that is different from what you believed 10 years ago?

3) Have you ever changed your political view on any issue?

4) Name two things that would have worked out better if you thought differently.

5) How important is God in your life?

8

HOW TO SET A NEW COURSE FOR YOUR LIFE

3) Behold, we put bits in the horses' mouths, that they may obey us; and we turn about their whole body. 4) Behold also the ships, which though they be so great, and are driven of fierce winds, yet are they turned about with a very small helm, whithersoever the governor listeth. 5) Even so the tongue is a little member, and boasteth great things. Behold, how great a matter a little fire kindleth!

James 3:3-5

When I was a child there was a proverb saying, "Sticks and stones may break my bones, but names will never hurt me". This turns out to be quite untrue. As a matter of fact, according to the epistle of James, words determine the direction our life. Words can affect our mood, our emotions, and even our health. There is no way you can achieve great things without speaking great words. Depending on your religious or philosophical background, this process has many names: reciting catechisms, confessions or faith declarations. What you call it is not quite as important as that you do it. You need to compose a list of the things you desire to see in your life; then, begin to craft your declarations in the affirmative. An example would be, " All my bills are paid, and I handle money wisely." Notice that I include the phrase "I handle money wisely." In order to change you need to change your actions well as your thinking. If we are honest with ourselves, we would admit that most of our debts are the byproduct of unwise spending. So, by including this phrase, you will begin to program your thinking; i.e., renew your mind to the wise handling of money.

The same process can be employed in building relationships, establishing healthy exercise routines, and developing whatever habits are essential for you to achieve your goals. Never underestimate the value of words. Words paint pictures, and the more words we use in the process of painting that picture, the more real that picture becomes. There are hundreds of studies that show when a hospital patient keeps repeating how bad he feels, the worse he actually does feel. Scientists believe that what we articulate on a consistent basis programs our minds to produce that program.

I challenge you to start this process tomorrow. When you wake up, say, "Today is going to be a great day. I will achieve all that I set out to do. At the end of this day, I will be satisfied, knowing I have accomplished great things. This was a great day!". If you do this each morning of the next seven days, I guarantee you will notice a difference in both your productivity, and outlook on each of those seven days.

The fact that you are reading this book tells me you have a strong desire to see things changed in your life.

Most people have no idea how important their vocabulary is in changing their life. I once lost over $10,000, because my vocabulary did not contain two words"stop loss". If these two words had been part of my financial vocabulary, months of planning,saving, and stock executions would have paid off in sizable dividends. The only way to turn a situation such as this around is to treat the event as a learning process, pay your tuition (the money lost), and learn; i.e., increase your vocabulary.

It will be impossible for you to escape from "Here" if your vocabulary is limited to the "Here" dictionary. Such words as "cannot", "do not know how", "that is impossible", "no one else is doing it"are evidence of speaking from the "Here" dictionary.

So, starting today you will develop and cultivate the vocabulary of where you want to be. If you are having financial problems, then buy a financial dictionary. If you have weight problems, buy a book on health and nutrition. If you are having trouble with your job, purchase books that address improving your worth to your employer.

Questions:

1) What are three things you say about yourself that you hope are not true?
2) How often do you say negative things about the people you have a relationship with?
3) Besides reading this book what actions have been taken in the last six months to improve your life?
4) Where would you like to be two years from today?
5) Name two things that occupy your time that you are willing to give up in order to set a new course for your life.

9

WORDS

"You will never progress beyond the words you use. " J. Woods

All of creation operates according to a set of laws. We call them "the laws of nature".

What few people understand is that nature not only functions by what we define as visible, measurable and quantifiable laws, but there is also a higher invisible law at work undergirding visible ones. This higher invisible law is responsible for nature itself. You can operate successfully following all the visible laws and yet fail in life because you violated the invisible law. You may think that this is unfair. How can you be expected to obey an invisible law? The answer, though you may not like it, is to understand who made and enforces this invisible law. Without this information your best efforts will always fall short.

The earth, just like your car, cell phone and a microwave oven, is a manufactured product. As such, just like them, it comes with an owner's manual to help you properly operate and maintain it. Many people drive their cars, use their cell phones, and operate the microwave without ever using the owner's manual. However, just as soon as a warning light comes on, they search for the owner's manual to see what the manufacturer recommends. But, many people never think to do that with other areas of life.

There has been provided for us an owner's manual produced by the manufacturer to guide us in the proper procedures for operating in this life. It is the Bible. Many people own a Bible and never think it pertains to everyday life. The Bible clearly provides instruction on how to operate in both the visible and invisible laws of creation. What is this invisible law, and how can I learn use it to facilitate success in life? Good question! To answer it will require going to the Bible itself.

The place to start is in the book of Genesis chapter 1 verses one through three.

1. In the beginning God created the heaven and the earth. 2. And the earth was without form, and void; and darkness was upon the face of the deep. And the Spirit of God moved upon the face of the waters. 3. And God said, Let there be light: and there was light.

The Bible clearly states that God is the manufacturer of all creation. As such, he knows how it is designed to function. I want to pay special attention to verse three. Notice it says "and God said". Nothing happened until God started speaking. All of creation came into existence with words. The invisible law that controls all of creation is the law of words. All of creation has been manufactured and designed to respond to the proper words.

22 And Jesus answering saith unto them, Have faith in God. 23 For verily I say unto you, That whosoever shall say unto this mountain, Be thou removed, and be thou cast into the sea; and shall not doubt in his heart, but shall believe that those things which he saith shall come to pass; he shall have whatsoever he saith. (Mark 11:22-23)

Jesus makes it clear that words, spoken in faith, can move mountains. If words can move mountains, they can move any other thing in creation, both seen and unseen. The real problem with any law is that it works all the time for good or bad. The law governing electricity will light your house or start your car, but it will also electrocute you, if you are not careful. It does not stop working just because you put yourself in the wrong position in relationship to its operation. Many of the problems people face in life are because of the operation of this law in a negative way. Jesus made it clear that if you believe what you say, that is what you will have . If you say "I will never get out of debt" and believe what you say, you will never get out of debt. If you say, "Every time I get ahead, things always set me back", you will get what you say. Creation and circumstances have been designed to obey faith-filled words.

Your physical body, including the central nervous system, immune system and brain, as created things respond to words. The words you choose to use can affect your health and longevity. Doctors have learned that patients who talk negatively about their health have measurable declines in their condition. Some studies have shown that the immune system will stop fighting certain diseases. They also determined that patients who speak optimistically have shorter recovery periods after major operations. This law is already at work in your life whether you believe it or not. Your current situations are in part the byproduct of your own words. Just like your mouth got you into this mess, your mouth can get you out.

A bit in the mouth of a horse controls the whole horse. A small rudder on a huge ship in the hands of a skilled captain sets a course in the face of the strongest winds. A word out of your mouth may seem of no account, but it can accomplish nearly anything—or destroy it! (James 3:3-5 The Message Bible)

The Bible makes it clear, that the words out of your mouth, just like the rudder of a ship, can and does set the course of your life. Your words can help you get where you want to go, or can destroy your best intentions. It is in your best interests to learn how to use your words to set the correct course of your life. To begin with you need to make a list of the things to stop saying. For example: Stop saying "I can't". This is one of the most destructive phrases in English. Train yourself to respond differently in situations you perceive to be a challenge. The correct response is "I can do all things through Christ who strengthens me". I would like to recommend you to read "The Tongue: a Creative Force" by Charles Capps.

Questions:
1) Have you ever purchased a new product and never looked at the owner's manual?
2) Have you ever been in a situation where you needed to check the owner's manual ?
3) Have you ever received an electrical shock?
4) Name three areas in which you might be violating the invisible law of words.

5) What are some words or phrases you use that may have led to your current situation?

6) As a result of this chapter, what changes are you making in the words you speak?

7) What steps are you taking to improve your vocabulary?

8) What is the most important thing you learned about words?

10

GOAL SETTING

Then the Lord answered me, "Write the vision. Make it clear on tablets so that anyone can read it quickly."

Habakkuk 2:2
God's Word Translation

> -" If you do not have a ring and a date you are not engaged; you are just on layaway." J. Woods

The true purpose of an engagement ring is to show a willingness to commit at a price. The purpose of the date is to add urgency and a deadline that forces action. In other words, a ring and the date set the goal and requires forward mobility. It is not enough to have both of these. You must put in writing a list of things to accomplish and the deadline at which to have it done. So it is with escaping from "Here". Set a deadline and pay the price of commitment. All the best ideas in the world are worthless, if they stay in your head and are never committed to paper. One reason to commit your goals to paper is that things sound differently in our heads than they do when in print. A true goal must be measurable and have a time limit. It must be easy to understand, so that even someone who does not know can read it.

Today you will write down your goals for leaving "Here". What will it take, and how long will it take? Be realistic, and understand that it may not be practical to leave "Here" overnight.

You will need to establish interim objectives to reach your long-term goal. For example: If you are deep in debt, you will need to establish a systematic plan for paying off your debts quickly. Depending on your income this may take a while. You will need to stop creating new debt to help facilitate the elimination of current debt. Therefore, your first objectives will be NO NEW DEBT!

From here you can establish other objectives that will lead you to your ultimate goal and deadline. Make multiple copies of your goals and objectives, and put them in key places around your home and place of work. You should read your goals aloud at least three times a day. This will keep you from conveniently forgetting your desire to get out of "Here". There are a plethora of books and online resources that will help you cultivate proper goal-setting skills. You just need to be willing to invest both time and money into your future. Freedom has never been free. But this I promise you, if you pay the price you will get to enjoy the price being paid. As a matter of fact, I recommend that you invest 5% of your earnings in improving your job skills, communication skills, or financial skills every year. This will cause you to be unlike anyone living in "Here", and make it almost impossible for you to live here ever again.

When you have established your goals and short-term objectives, and have them in writing, you will be well on your way to an effective escape. Do not allow mistakes, missed deadlines or blatant failures to keep your word, hinder you from the life you and your family truly deserve. The truth is, there are things we would be willing to do for the sake of our children, but would not do for ourselves. So, whatever it takes to motivate, push your buttons, give you backbone or move you to action, do it! I look forward to seeing you anywhere but "Here". Questions:

1) Before reading this book, did you have any goals in writing? If so, what were they ?

2) List three things you would like to accomplish in the next year.

3) List the first thing you would need to do to begin accomplishing each one.

4) Do you presently own any books on goal setting?

5) When was the last time you set a goal and reached it?

6) Write down a brief description of what your life will be like one year from today. Include in this list how you feel, how much money you have in bank, where you will live and who you will work for.

11

PACK YOUR BAGS!
YOU'RE OUT OF "HERE"!

You have come to the point where it is time to go. Put the house up for sale, cancel your subscriptions, pack the boxes and send the deposit to the moving company, because today you are out of "Here"! You have wasted too much time in this city, and it has consumed too much of your resources. Both you and your family deserve better than this, and it is time that you draw the line in the sand and go.

By now you understand there are only two ways to escape the city: you have to fly, or you have to sail. So, unless you have airline tickets or cruise tickets, you are not leaving. The way you acquire these tickets is by obeying the laws of words, changing your thinking, setting written goals and implementing them. You may also need to disassociate yourself from people and situations that make you feel comfortable with living "Here".

You and your family will need to cultivate the vocabulary of where you are moving to, and abandon your "Here" vocabulary and accent. You may have to dress differently and deny yourself many of the luxuries that trap people "Here". But because you are ready to leave, you will have no problem with any of this. Your biggest challenge is overcoming the voices of the inhabitants of "Here". They will tug at your heartstrings and your fears as they attempt to transfer their fears to you. Because the truth is as you succeed you shine light on their failure. Do not underestimate their determination and resourcefulness. The one thing that they fear more than anything else is watching people escape. So they will do anything to keep you and your family in the same captivity from which you see no way out. As a matter of fact, one of the best strategies is to convince you of all the dangers that await, and if you loved your family you are not subject to such risk. Do not fall for it!

If you have planned your escape properly and worked your plan correctly, you will ignore all their voices. The best way to do this is to remind yourself and your family of all the benefits that will be enjoyed upon escaping. This can be accomplished by having a dream board with pictures from magazines depicting your new lifestyle. Every day, before your escape, you need to look at this board and discuss all the wonderful things it contains. Carry in your pocket a daily affirmation of your new lifestyle and read it no less than three times each day. Talk to other escapees and listen to how the vocabulary and diction is different. Collect and read publications on travel and success.

You deserve and have been designed by God to enjoy His very best. It is up to you, not Him, to take any steps and make any changes necessary for you to fulfill and satisfy all requirements to partake of what awaits you. What you have read in this book is the beginning of your journey, but it is by no means the end. Only you can determine how far you go and how much you accomplish. The only limits are the ones you set. Others are depending on you to show the way. We who have already escaped look forward to spending time with you and hearing your testimony.

Questions:

1)   What would be an example of how you could pack your bags?

2)   Write an affirmation describing your new lifestyle. Include the things you want, such as: job,income and housing.

3)   Has anyone ever tried to talk you out of leaving your current situation for a better one? They will.

CPSIA information can be obtained at www.ICGtesting.com
Printed in the USA
BVOW06s1534260416

445599BV00003BA/4/P